# ROCKET MAN

# ROCKET MAN

## The Story of Robert Goddard

### TOM STREISSGUTH

Carolrhoda Books, Inc./Minneapolis

*To Adele*

The publisher wishes to thank Dorothy E. Mosakowski, Coordinator of Archives and Special Collections, Robert Hutchings Goddard Library, Clark University, for her help with the preparation of this book.

Carolrhoda Books, Inc. c/o The Lerner Group
241 First Avenue North, Minneapolis, MN 55401

Library of Congress Cataloging-in-Publication Data

Streissguth, Thomas, 1958–
    Rocket man : the story of Robert Goddard / Tom Streissguth.
        p. cm.
    Includes bibliographical references and index.
    ISBN 0-87614-863-1
    1. Goddard, Robert Hutchings, 1882–1945—Juvenile literature.
2. Rocketry—United States—Biography—Juvenile literature. [1. Goddard, Robert Hutchings, 1882–1945. 2. Physicists. 3. Rocketry.] I. Title.
TL781.85.G6S77 1995
621.43'56'092—dc20
[B]                                                                94-22836
                                                                         CIP
                                                                          AC

Manufactured in the United States of America
1 2 3 4 5 6 I/JR 00 99 98 97 96 95

# Contents

Robert Goddard, age ten, with his parents, Nahum and Fanny
Goddard, at their home in Worcester, Massachusetts

# A Curious
# Boy

One...two...three...

The boy was peering down into a basin of water, counting the small, black flecks of...what? He stared, trying to focus his eyes, and paid no attention to the tube of hydrogen in his right hand. The tube moved closer to an open flame that sputtered from a Bunsen burner.

Four...five...BANG!

The tube touched the flame and suddenly exploded with a terrifying crack of shattered glass. Jagged slivers shot upward into the ceiling and across the room into the wall. The noise rattled the windowpanes and seemed to shake the room and the entire house.

Outside, in the hall, a maid fainted to the floor.

Nahum and Fanny Goddard came running into the room. Robert, their sixteen-year-old son, was sitting calmly at his worktable, inspecting his hands and clothing for damage. It was just an experiment, he explained. He was just trying to make diamonds.

He had read about it in a book. They had figured out a way to manufacture diamonds, which were simply hard crystals of a natural element called carbon. Graphite is also made of carbon, but in a softer form. Maybe, he thought, there was some way to crystallize graphite. A sudden change in temperature might work. Perhaps he could do it on his own.

He had heated a heavy lump of iron and graphite over a flame fed by hydrogen and oxygen gas. He waited until the lump was too hot to handle, then threw it into a basin of cold water. He was peering down intently at the steaming water and had forgotten all about the tube of explosive hydrogen—and the dangerous open flame.

Fanny offered her son a broom and a dustpan. This wasn't the first of his experiments, and she knew it wouldn't be the last. Robert cleaned up the broken glass, turned off the burner, and emptied the basin. As the water drained from the basin, he discovered that the flecks from the heated graphite stone had indeed changed. They had turned into...cold graphite.

The maid revived, surprised to discover that she was still alive. Mr. and Mrs. Goddard ordered an immediate stop to any future diamond experiments.

Robert was their only child, born on October 5, 1882. He was old enough by now for high school, but too sick with colds and bronchitis to attend classes every day. So he spent most of his time at home, reading library books. He was teaching himself about electricity, physics, and chemistry.

He was curious and eager to learn how things worked

and how they were put together. Nahum Goddard encouraged his son by giving him a telescope and a microscope. The Goddards had also bought electric lights for the house and one of the first gasoline-powered automobiles ever seen in Roxbury, Massachusetts.

Every month, _Scientific American_ arrived at the Goddard house. The magazine described amazing inventions and daring, dangerous experiments. Robert and Nahum carefully studied the magazine's articles and complex drawings, which described the new telephones, phonographs, and crystal radio sets. Nahum had even created a few inventions of his own. One of them was a knife that would cut cleanly through the thick, soft fur of rabbits.

Nahum liked his independence. In 1883, a few months after his son had been born, he had quit his job as an accountant. He had moved his family from Worcester, a town about forty miles west of Boston, to Roxbury, a suburb of the big coastal city. With his partner Simeon Stubbs, he had founded Stubbs and Goddard, a company that made specially designed knives used to cut paper, wood, and other materials. The job demanded time, travel, and salesmanship.

The business was successful. But in 1898, Fanny Goddard came down with tuberculosis, a dangerous lung disease. The family doctor advised Nahum to move his family out of Roxbury and to a healthier, drier climate. Nahum sold his interest in Stubbs and Goddard. The family packed their bags and belongings and moved back to Maple Hill, their place in Worcester.

The backyard of Maple Hill, the Goddard family's home in Worcester. As a boy, Robert spent many hours here when he was too ill to go to school.

Robert didn't mind moving. The house at Maple Hill had big rooms, an upstairs workshop, and a wide front porch. Best of all, it had a large backyard with plenty of space for his experiments. It had a shed for his tools and ladders and a small creek nearby. Near the creek was a spindly cherry tree.

Very soon, this frail old tree would change Robert's life forever.

# A Gifted
# Student

Robert was sick with bronchitis, and home from school again.

The long hours of morning, afternoon, and evening stretched out before him, promising little. When darkness fell, there would be another long night of restless sleep. As he tried to make a plan for the day, he strained to breathe the stale, damp air. A deep, hollow cough rose up from his chest. There was little he could do. The doctors had told him to stay inside, rest, and try to recover his strength.

The *Boston Post* had arrived at the house. Tired of reading library books, Robert picked up the newspaper. Between the articles describing business deals and sports contests were photos of criminals, politicians, and celebrities. There was nothing to interest him except for a story called "The War of the Worlds." The newspaper was printing, chapter by chapter, this science-fiction tale by the famous English writer H.G. Wells.

A hostile army of Martians had sailed through the cold, black, airless vacuum of outer space and landed on planet Earth. Their spaceships were armed with a powerful heat ray that could destroy anything in its path. They would enslave the Earth's entire population—starting with the people of Boston.

Fascinated, Robert read each of the new installments as they appeared in the *Post*. He wasn't afraid of Martians, or heat rays, or interplanetary wars. He knew that Earth's enslavement by alien beings was just a figment of the author's overworked imagination. But this fantastic, unbelievable story made him wonder. *How did that spaceship work?*

Could a human being fly into space?

He thought about it, turning the possibilities over and over in his mind. Perhaps it could be done with a gunpowder rocket. But to escape the pull of earth's gravity—the force that kept people and things firmly on the ground—this rocket would need to go 25,000 miles per hour. In order to have enough power to reach this speed, the rocket would have to carry hundreds of pounds of heavy gunpowder. And the heavier the load, the more gunpowder would be needed to get the rocket off the ground. The more gunpowder, the heavier the load... and...well....

One clear and warm October day in 1899, he walked out of the back door of the house and into the yard. He was feeling strong enough to do a little working instead of studying. After getting a saw and a ladder from the toolshed, he climbed into the small cherry tree and began pruning its branches. It was a slow and easy task, and his mind began to wander.

He saw something above his head. It was a small device that was spinning and lifting itself into the blue sky. The device was escaping the pull of gravity. It was heading straight up into the sky.

The yard was quiet except for the sound of an autumn breeze. The sky was clear, and empty. Robert knew he had imagined something—but what? He climbed out of the tree, put the saw and the ladder away, and went back into the house. In the diary he was keeping, he would mark that day—October 19—every year, for the rest of his life.

He returned to school, and the *Post* printed its last installment of "The War of the Worlds." He could gather visions in his head and dream some other time. First he had to graduate.

He worked hard to pass the difficult math and science courses at South High School. Although Robert had missed quite a few school days in the past few years, he soon caught up with his classmates. He was especially good at math and physics. He could read the problems set out by his teachers and quickly grasp the key to answering them.

Mr. Andrews, the physics teacher, saw promise in this eager student. The teacher and his pupil became friends. After school, they spent time together, talking things over. Robert had a lot of questions for his teacher on the subject of flying into space.

How could a pilot stay alive in space, where there

was no air to breathe? Could a rocket make it past the strong pull of Earth's gravity? How could it slow down, and how could it land again? How long would it take to fly a hundred million miles to the planet Mars? Mr. Andrews was a good teacher, but he couldn't answer these questions. He never even thought about space-flight. Nobody did!

Robert studied hard, trying to come up with a way to get his imaginary rockets into the air. He took notes and made calculations in his diary. He read books about famous scientists to see if anybody else might have posed the same questions and come up with answers. In a book by Sir Isaac Newton, a famous English physicist, he read this:

"To every action there is always opposed an equal re-action: or the mutual actions of two bodies upon each other are aways equal, and directed to contrary parts."

According to this Third Law, one object reacting against another would go in a different direction from that object. A rocket could thus react against the burning of fuel that was directed downward, toward the ground. Newton's law said that the rocket would then go in the opposite direction: upward.

A lightweight fuel that burned slowly and steadily could put his craft into orbit. The steady burning would enable the rocket to gradually reach escape velocity (the speed needed to escape the pull of gravity). But gunpowder burned all at once with the force of an uncontrolled ex-

Robert at his graduation from South High School in Worcester, in 1904

plosion. Rockets needed a fuel that would provide a continuous reaction, a smooth acceleration. If gunpowder didn't work, what would?

In 1904 Robert finally graduated from high school, at the top of his class. He was twenty-one years old. Although he had spent a lot of time on the problem of spaceflight, he was not even close to a solution. His ideas and problems and notes, and conversations with Mr. Andrews, hadn't helped much. All his classes at South High, and all the books he had been studying, seemed to state the dry, discouraging fact. Spaceflight was impossible.

One day that summer, he collected all his notes on rockets and space travel and fuels and placed them inside the living room stove. He lit a match, tossed it into the stove, and closed the heavy iron door. The papers burned brightly, turned to blackened ash, and floated up into the sky. His questions had no answers, and it was time to turn to a more practical problem—the problem of his future.

# 3.

# Dreams of Flight

Robert soon discovered that his impractical dream refused to fly away with the ashes of his burned notebooks. A few days later, he was writing again in a new book. For now, he would have to study and learn. He needed to know physics, mathematics, chemistry, and astronomy. There were formulas, equations, and scientific laws to understand. He needed to find the ideal rocket fuel and create a lightweight metal for his spacecraft.

But it was also time to learn something useful. Nahum Goddard was not a wealthy man, and he couldn't pay for expensive schooling. So Mary Goddard, Robert's grandmother, agreed to borrow enough money to send her grandson to Worcester Polytechnic Institute, a school for civil engineers.

At the Tech, students learned to design buildings, bridges, and machinery. There was much to learn in only a few years, and there would be no mention of space-flight, rockets, or the works of H.G. Wells. In class, Robert kept his dream to himself.

But in his notebooks and diaries, he worked out hundreds of ideas and possibilities. In 1906 he considered solar energy—power from the sun—as a fuel source for his spaceship. In 1907 he thought about launching the craft from a high-flying balloon, in order to give it a head start into space. In 1908 he worked out a plan for exploring the moon's dark side, which was never visible from the earth.

By 1909 he had decided that a modified artillery rocket would have the best chance to escape the pull of gravity. Although gunpowder rockets had been used by the world's armies for centuries for signaling and as weapons, they were no longer used in those ways. They burned uncontrollably and couldn't match the accuracy and power of heavy guns.

Spaceflight, however, was not war. Robert's main concern was to lift his rocket beyond the atmosphere. Finding the right fuel was the key to solving the problem.

His chemistry books seemed to say that the perfect fuel for a space rocket would be liquid hydrogen and liquid oxygen. The liquid hydrogen would be the propellant, the fuel that would make the rocket move. It would burn steadily and provide the maximum amount of thrust, or upward power. Liquid oxygen would take the place of the air needed to keep the fuel burning, since there would be no air in space. But these were expensive and dangerous substances. They would be difficult to use in experiments.

Once in a while, Robert had a chance to work out his ideas for a class. For an assignment on travel in the year

1950, he described a train that could travel from New York to Boston in a vacuum tube. The train would be powered by an electric current. Since there would be no rails and no air in the tube, there would be no friction or air resistance to slow the train down. The trip would take ten minutes instead of several hours.

For an English class, he wrote an essay on the gyroscope, a device made up of spinning wheels that helped airplanes to steer and to keep their balance. The paper impressed his teacher, who suggested that Robert send it to *Scientific American.* The magazine accepted the piece and published it.

Robert had less luck with an essay called "On the Possibility of Navigating Interplanetary Space." He sent this paper to *Scientific American* as well as *Popular Astronomy,* but both magazines turned him down. They dealt with facts, not fantasy, and the idea of navigating interplanetary space was fit only for fiction writers like H.G. Wells.

Robert worked hard at his major subject, electrical engineering, and again finished at the top of his class. Worcester Polytechnic awarded him a prize of seventy-five dollars at his graduation ceremony in the spring of 1908. He enrolled that fall at Clark University in Worcester. In just three years, he earned a doctorate in physics, the study of matter, energy, and the natural laws that made the world work. After seven years of college, he had become Dr. Robert Goddard.

After Goddard's graduation, Clark offered him a position as an "honorary fellow." This meant that although there would be no salary, he could use the university's laboratories for his research. For the next year, he worked on an important problem of electrical engineering: how to measure an electric current flowing through a vacuum tube. He came up with a new measurement device called a vacuum tube oscillator.

Goddard's study of electricity earned him some attention among his fellow scientists. When officials from Harvard University asked him to make a speech about his research, Goddard agreed.

In the audience that night sat Dr. W. F. Magie, a dean of Princeton University, in New Jersey. Impressed with Goddard's knowledge and great skill in the laboratory,

Robert studied vacuum tubes as part of his research into the possibility of spaceflight. Here he holds a circular vacuum tube outside the physics shop at Clark University.

Dean Magie offered him a job as a research instructor. There would be plenty of time for research, and a regular salary. Goddard gladly accepted for the term beginning in the fall of 1912, when he would turn thirty years old.

At Princeton, Goddard continued his electrical experiments. But he also worked on a set of calculations for the rocket that he had yet to build.

Early in the spring of 1913, a bad cold interrupted his work. High fevers and coughing fits made it impossible to teach, write, or think. During a school break, Goddard went home to Worcester.

A group of doctors came to examine him at Maple Hill. Robert and his family feared the worst, and the worst came true. The diagnosis was tuberculosis, the same disease that had infected Fanny Goddard. After finishing the examination, the doctors left their patient and moved to another room, where they spoke together in low voices. They all agreed that the case was a serious one. The disease had come on suddenly and was spreading rapidly. Dr. Goddard, in their opinion, had about two weeks to live.

# Figuring
# It Out

The doctors advised Goddard to stay quiet and to avoid exercise of any kind. They said his lungs might heal if he slept outside on the porch, in the cold March air. But even if he managed to survive, he would still carry the tuberculosis bacteria. He might live longer, they told him, if he moved to a drier, sunnier climate and avoided stressful work.

But the patient had ideas of his own. At night he slept in his warm room; after sunrise he walked outside as much as he could. To keep his strength up, Goddard strolled up the slope of a nearby hill. Every day, he managed to walk a little bit farther. Two weeks passed, and he remained alive. But his recovery took more than a year.

Goddard had his papers and books brought back from Princeton. He kept his notes under his pillow and worked on them from time to time, careful to keep them out of

Robert Goddard teaching a physics class at Clark University

sight. The doctors arrived regularly, made their exami-
nations, and left. Gradually, their opinions changed. He
would survive after all.

When he felt well enough, Goddard returned to Clark
University and began teaching a course in electricity. He
explained charges, currents, ions and electrons, voltages
and vacuum tubes and electrical resistance. His lectures

in this strange and difficult new science were clear and detailed. At the end of his courses, his students cheered him from their seats.

In his office and his laboratory, he was studying a very different science, one that was even younger and more uncertain. He was very careful with the packages of rockets that arrived in heavy, protective wrapping. There were Chinese rockets, British Congreve rockets, signal rockets, fireworks, and flares. He cut them open to examine their fuses and charges. On the grounds of the Clark campus, he fired off the rockets to learn exactly how they flew. He posed himself a question: Could these devices possibly be modified for spaceflight?

The heavy black gunpowder packed into the rockets contained an explosive mixture of chemicals—sulfur, charcoal, and potassium nitrate. When the gunpowder was lit, the burning gases rapidly expanded inside the rockets and then escaped downward through nozzles. As Newton's Third Law predicted, the rocket then reacted by moving in the opposite direction, away from the ground and into the sky.

Goddard also carefully examined the rockets to learn how their shape and design helped them to fly. All of them were cylinders. They were tapered at the top, smooth and straight along the sides, and flat at the bottom, where the exhaust gases were forced outward. With his study, Goddard discovered a very important principle of rocket propulsion: The narrower the nozzle at the bottom, the more pressure was created inside the rocket, and the greater the thrust that powered it upward.

The British army used Congreve rockets, which carried explosives, to attack U.S. forces at Fort McHenry, Maryland, during the War of 1812.

But even though narrow nozzles could create more lifting power, the rockets that Goddard examined would never get very far off the ground. The solid fuels were hard to control, they were heavy, and they burned inefficiently. Just as he had thought, liquid hydrogen and oxygen were the answer.

But liquid hydrogen was impossible to find, and liquid oxygen was expensive. Lox, as it was called, had to be kept in special vacuum tanks at a temperature of $-297°$ F to remain in liquid form. If the temperature rose any higher, the lox would turn from a liquid into a useless gas. Goddard didn't have the money to buy lox or the equipment needed to handle it. For the time being, he would have to work with solid fuels.

In his workshop, he began building his first rockets and searching for the most efficient method of burning solid propellants. The rockets were about a foot long, and an inch thick, and made of steel. Inside the devices, he assembled a maze of tubing and valves that would hold the fuel and control how it was burned.

The fuels—gunpowder and other solid powders—were placed in separate cartridges. Like the bullets in a revolver, the cartridges were injected one by one into a combustion chamber, where they would ignite. He linked the combustion chamber to an exhaust nozzle, a smooth-sided tube that flared outward underneath the body of the rocket. The gases would flow through the tube and out of the rocket.

Goddard built a steel frame to hold the rockets in place during ignition. When he was confident that the rockets would actually get off the ground, he brought them outside for test flights. During one of these tests, a small steel rocket reached a height of 486 feet. The cartridge-feeding system, as he had designed it, was burning the solid fuels more efficiently than a simple explosion would have.

Goddard worked in secrecy and spoke to few people of his invention. Worried about losing his ideas and designs to another inventor, or to a commercial business, he decided to patent several versions of his small rockets.

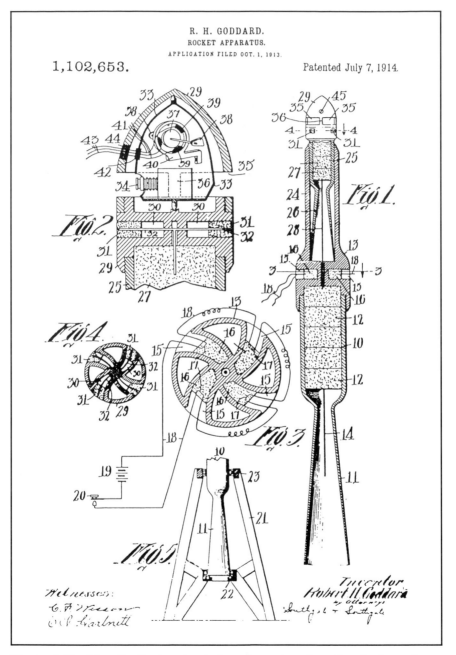

Part of Goddard's first patent drawing, showing the designs for a small rocket fired by solid fuels

Charles T. Hawley, a Worcester patent lawyer, agreed to prepare drawings that showed Goddard's rocket design and send them with an application to the U.S. Patent Office. In 1914 the office awarded two patents—numbers 1,102,653 and 1,103,503—on the "Goddard rocket."

The patent designs showed a rocket combustion chamber, in which fuels would burn, and a rocket nozzle, through which the exhaust gases would be propelled outward. Goddard also described a multiple-stage rocket. This would have a primary stage, or section, with a combustion chamber and a fuel tank, and a secondary stage that would separate from the primary when the fuel was used up.

The patents meant that, for a period of seventeen years, the designs belonged exclusively to Robert Goddard. No one else could copy, manufacture, or sell them without Goddard's permission. This was Goddard's way of protecting himself, a method he had learned from his inventive, practical father. With the perfection of each new device, Nahum Goddard's son would pay a visit to the offices of Charles T. Hawley, who would file the necessary papers for a new patent.

The patents brought Goddard no money, however, because there was no commercial use for the Goddard rocket. It was a laboratory device, simply a way to demonstrate his theories. It couldn't carry messages, harvest crops, or dig for gold. It was impractical—just a product of his own curiosity.

Goddard had to rely on his salary as a teacher to buy materials, and money was always short. In 1916 he turned to the Smithsonian Institution in Washington D.C. for help. This was an institute for scientific research, which funded many different projects and experiments.

Goddard claimed that his rockets could be used for raising weather recording devices, such as thermometers and barometers, high into the earth's atmosphere. His calculations showed that the Goddard rocket could possibly reach an altitude ten times higher than the highest research balloons.

It was all set out in detail in a paper he had written: "A Method of Reaching Extreme Altitudes." Goddard sent his paper to the Smithsonian and also appealed to the chief of the army's ordnance department, which bought artillery and ammunition for the military. Goddard asked for support for the building of a long-range artillery rocket.

Impressed by Goddard's claims, the Smithsonian granted him five thousand dollars in the next year. The Army Signal Corps also agreed to help him with a grant of twenty thousand dollars. Both donors were eager to see Goddard make something useful out of his ideas and theories. The professor used some of the money to hire several assistants and moved into a small workshop on the campus of the Worcester Polytechnic Institute.

By this time, the United States had entered World War I against Germany, and Goddard was worried about enemy spies. He covered the windows of his new shop with blankets and hired a night watchman. But it still wasn't enough for him. Curious people haunted the premises, and streetcars rattled the windows and walls.

With the help of the military, Goddard moved his operation to Mount Wilson, the site of an observatory near Los Angeles, California.

By November 1918, Goddard was ready to show his weapons. He had developed a portable rocket-launching tube that soldiers could easily handle. With the help of an assistant, Clarence Hickman, he arranged for a demonstration at an army firing range. The two men set up the tube launcher on a pair of music stands. They then fired off several shells, which streaked out of the tubes and demolished the heavy sandbags that served as targets. The launcher and the music stands didn't budge.

The officers who attended the demonstration were quite impressed by what they saw. Unlike other artillery weapons, Goddard's tube launchers had no recoil or "kick," which made them easier and safer to use. They could be carried and fired off by foot soldiers. The generals and admirals promised to continue helping Goddard with money and research facilities.

But a few days after the demonstration, Germany surrendered and the war was over. There was no need for tube launchers, much less for high-flying rockets. And there would be no more money from the military for Goddard's research.

# Lift Off

Goddard was back at Clark University, where he had become a senior member of the physics department. His classes and his research were going well, and his private life was changing. He had met a younger woman named Esther Kisk, a secretary in the president's office. Soon Esther was helping Professor Goddard type his notes and research articles.

The two became friends, much to the dismay of Esther's strict parents. Although Esther went away to college in Maine, the professor didn't forget about her. She was one of the few people who didn't see his work on rockets as an impossible flight of fancy. In June 1924, Robert and Esther were married.

In the laboratory, Goddard tinkered with his rocket motors and fuel tanks, trying to overcome the many problems of his cartridge-feeding system. As often as not, the valves and tubes would jam, or break, or fail to ignite. There were many moving parts and just as many ways for the hot, expanding gases inside the rocket to cause some kind of breakdown of the equipment.

But Goddard would not give up. He made more calculations and changes, and filled the lab with the loud whirr of machinery, the fumes of burning gunpowder, and the steady scream of igniting rocket motors. The work and noise impressed Goddard's fellow professors as well as Dr. Arthur Webster, the head of the physics department at Clark.

Dr. Webster and Dr. Goddard were friends, but they had their differences. Webster was a brilliant mathematician whose experiments and theories were all set down in writing. His workshop was made up of classroom blackboards, lecture notes, and articles that he published in scientific journals. Goddard's notion of high-altitude flight was a practical goal, but one that he wanted to protect from copycats and rivals.

Webster did not believe in keeping scientific research a secret. He insisted that his colleague publish his findings. If Goddard didn't publish, Webster claimed he would write up Goddard's findings and publish them himself. Goddard would get the proper credit for his work—but he would also get plenty of publicity.

Goddard resisted. He wanted to keep working quietly until he had reached his goal. But he couldn't let Webster upstage him, and as an employee of Webster's he couldn't simply refuse. So he agreed to publish a second version of "A Method of Reaching Extreme Altitudes," the essay on rocket flight that he had written several years before. He sent the paper to the Smithsonian.

One paragraph that Goddard added to the paper was just a vague idea. One day, he wrote, it would be possible to send a rocket as far as the moon. The craft might carry a gunpowder charge that would go off when the rocket reached its destination. The flash would be bright enough to be seen by telescopes on Earth.

The museum published 1,750 copies of Goddard's paper in December 1919. Most of the readers were scientists—the only audience that could understand Goddard's difficult theories and complicated math. But in the next month, the Smithsonian also sent out a notice about Goddard's paper to several newspapers. The notice claimed, in plain and simple English, that Goddard was preparing a rocket for a flight to the moon.

Perhaps the Smithsonian's directors were simply seeking some public attention in return for the money they had already invested in Goddard. They did indeed receive publicity—a sensational story splashed across the front page of every major newspaper in the country. The *New York Times* claimed:

## AIM TO REACH MOON WITH NEW ROCKET

Suddenly, rocket fever was sweeping the nation. Dr. Goddard, the shy and careful professor from Worcester, was now the famous Moon Rocket Man. Reporters called him to ask for more details of the coming spaceflights. Many people wrote Goddard to volunteer for the first ride to the moon.

The publicity, and the many errors printed in the news-

Goddard in the Clark physics shop, holding an early form of a rocket motor

papers, angered Goddard. Having people volunteer for the imagined first moon flight was bad enough. Even worse, many people were scorning him and trying to prove that his theories and dreams were impossible. Had they even bothered to read his paper?

On the other hand, Goddard did see an opportunity to raise more money for his research. He quickly suggested a public subscription of $100,000. Anyone could contribute to the fund, which would pay for the design and construction of a high-altitude rocket.

But when no more rocket news came from Worcester, the story rapidly disappeared from the papers and the public eye. People forgot about Goddard, and the moon-rocket subscription came to nothing. To replace the

Smithsonian grant, which Goddard had spent, Clark pitched in $3,500 for another two years of work.

Goddard was not the only scientist working on rocket flight. A German writer named Hermann Oberth had carefully read "A Method of Reaching Extreme Altitudes." Fascinated, he wrote a letter to Goddard in May 1922, offering to cooperate in developing a rocket. Goddard wrote back to Oberth, politely refusing to take on any partners.

In the next year, Oberth published *The Rocket Into Planetary Space,* a book that borrowed many of Goddard's own ideas on rocket construction. Oberth's letters and writings convinced Goddard that he was now in the middle of an international space race. Determined to build and launch a working model, he searched the countryside near Worcester to find a better site for his noisy

Hermann Oberth, pioneering German rocket engineer

test flights. In Auburn, about five miles from Worcester, he discovered a large, empty field on the property of Effie Ward, a distant relative of the Goddard family.

Realizing that solid fuels would never succeed in reaching high altitudes, he had switched to liquid fuels. For ten dollars, he could buy two liters of liquid oxygen from a local welding company. Since liquid hydrogen was unavailable, he substituted gasoline as the propellant.

He strengthened the valves and pumps in the rocket to withstand even higher temperatures. The combustion chamber was now made of duralumin, a metal made from copper, magnesium, manganese, and aluminum. Although the material was thin and lightweight, it could withstand heat that would rapidly melt most other common metals.

By late 1925, Goddard had finished a new rocket that measured about 10½ feet long and weighed about 10 pounds when loaded with fuel. A strange contraption of tubes and tanks, the rocket looked like the inside of a giant lightbulb. The long and thin tubes on the outside of the frame linked the rocket motor and nozzle, at the top of the device, with the fuel tanks, which were placed in the lower half. There was no outer shell covering the rocket, so these working parts could be plainly seen.

Goddard brought the device out to Effie Ward's farm. With his assistant Henry Sachs, he set up a launching frame made out of welded iron pipes. The frame held the rocket upright, pointed at the sky. Through the cold winter months, Goddard and Sachs carefully checked the fuel tanks and the steel tubing for leaks and cracks.

Goddard posed with his liquid-fueled rocket shortly before its launch on March 16, 1926.

Esther Goddard joined them, using a movie camera to record the tests.

On March 16, after several misfirings, Goddard prepared for another test. The day was clear and calm—good weather for another try. The professor opened a valve on the outside of the rocket. Liquid oxygen and gasoline began flowing into the combustion chamber. At the same time, Henry Sachs held a flaming blowtorch at the end of a long pole. Carefully, Sachs touched the flame of the torch to the rocket's motor.

Suddenly a hot, smokeless white flame sputtered out of the rocket's nozzle. Goddard held the release cord in his hand, waiting for the motor to build up power. After a minute, he pulled the cord. Nothing happened as the seconds slowly went by. Then the rocket and its fuel tanks began to lift themselves up and beyond the iron pipes of the launch frame.

The rocket accelerated to about 60 miles per hour, and gained 41 feet in altitude. Gravity fought with Goddard's motor, and then the craft began to heel over to the side. Finally, after a flight of 2½ seconds, it crashed back to the snow-covered ground, 184 feet away from the launch site.

It was the world's first flight of a liquid-fueled rocket. Goddard had taken the first small step in realizing his dream.

# Crashing and Burning

After the launch, Goddard examined the dented frame of his rocket and considered changing its design. In the workshop he moved the combustion chamber down below the fuel tanks, which would steady the rocket and, he hoped, lengthen the flight. He brought the rocket back out to Auburn on April 3. This time, the device flew for a little more than four seconds and landed about 50 feet away from the launch tower.

The two test flights over Effie Ward's farm had proved that liquid-fueled rockets *could* work. But Goddard's rockets were little more than fanciful gadgets; they would never achieve high-altitude flight. If he could design a rocket that could reach the height of 25 miles—the highest any gas balloon had so far reached—the fantasy of space exploration would become a possibility.

At least one thing stood in his way: money. Goddard did not have enough to buy the necessary materials and fuel. He was an inventor, not a salesman, although he had made a start by writing to Charles G. Abbott, assistant secretary at the Smithsonian. Abbott had obtained a $2,500 grant for Goddard through a private foundation.

Pleased with the tests at Auburn, and eager to see more successful flights, Abbott now asked Goddard how much more money he needed. The professor thought it over carefully and asked for a grant of $6,500, which he claimed might put a rocket into high-altitude flight in about a year. In July 1926, the Smithsonian approved the grant.

The solution to the problem seemed to be a much larger rocket, one that could hold more fuel. Goddard began designing a new combustion chamber and a larger frame. New fuel tanks were designed to hold twenty times as much propellant. Goddard also bought an abandoned windmill tower and moved it out to Aunt Effie's farm. The 60-foot tower would hold the larger rocket securely upright before liftoff.

On May 3, 1927, a little more than a year after the first liquid-fueled flight, a new rocket was ready for a test. Goddard and his crew hauled the craft out to the farm, set it up within the windmill tower, and prepared their cables and switches. A countdown began.

Five...four...three...two...one...

The rocket slowly lifted from the ground. But as it cleared the tower, there was a flash of bright light and a sharp noise. The gasoline tank had exploded.

There were several more tests that summer. But after each ignition, the rocket sat in its launch tower without budging. Since the rocket was much heavier now, it had

Goddard and his crew used this wagon to carry rocket test equipment to the launch site at Aunt Effie Ward's farm.

to carry more fuel, and burn the fuel at a higher temperature, to get off the ground.  But the higher temperatures were destroying the walls of the combustion chamber. Goddard would have to come up with a method of cooling the chamber—without adding much more weight to the rocket.

The professor calmly accepted his failures; he knew that there would be many more to come.  Each launch was an opportunity to learn from his mistakes and prepare for the necessary improvements.  Goddard also understood that the road he was traveling was a long and uncertain one.  There would be accidents and detours along the way—but he would never lose sight of his destination.

Despite the string of failures that summer, his sponsors at the Smithsonian decided to grant him another five thousand dollars for his work. Goddard used the money to build a new model with fewer parts. This rocket was 12 feet long and weighed 32 pounds, without fuel. During the summer and fall of 1928, the rocket was ignited four times at Auburn. Each time, either the valves or the combustion chamber burned out, and the rocket never cleared the launch tower.

On July 17, 1929, the rocket was again made ready for firing. For the first time, recording instruments—a camera and a barometer, used for measuring air pressure—were carried aboard. The rocket cleared the tower and rose 100 feet before the gas tank exploded.

The noise of the explosion and the impact of the falling rocket could be heard from miles away. Certain that a plane had crashed, several of Aunt Effie's frightened neighbors called the police. Police officers and newspaper reporters rushed out to the launch site. While Robert and Esther and the crew calmly examined the wreckage, the reporters asked questions and nosed around the launch tower.

The next day, the story hit the papers. Goddard had set off a rocket for the moon! During the next several weeks, hundreds of strangers arrived at the farm, eager to see another launch. Goddard was again making news.

But his test flights were now in trouble. The people of Auburn had decided that rocket testing was much too dangerous. The town asked Goddard to find another place to launch his rockets. Happy to escape the crowds and the publicity, Goddard packed up his equipment and moved to Camp Devens, an artillery range near Worcester.

Goddard valued his privacy above all. He believed in keeping his ideas to himself and protecting his inventions as well as he could. And he didn't care for fame. The newspapers were doing him more harm than good by writing about "flights to the moon." The more people expected from him, the harder it was to get any useful work done.

Perhaps the experiences of another pioneer in flight were teaching Goddard this hard lesson. In May 1927, the pilot Charles Lindbergh had become the first flyer to cross the Atlantic Ocean alone. The voyage from the United States to Paris took 33½ hours. Before Lindbergh's takeoff, most people believed such a flight was impossible. Several other pilots had already died trying it.

Charles Lindbergh with his history-making plane, the *Spirit of St. Louis*

Lindbergh had done the impossible, and after his landing in Paris, he became an international hero. He was honored with parades and medals and awards. He gave speeches, wrote books and articles, and answered thousands of questions from newspaper reporters.

In a few years, pilots were flying back and forth between Europe and the United States. The Atlantic crossing became normal, almost routine. Despite the expectations of more great things from him, Lindbergh could never again equal his courageous solo flight. The newspapers hounded him, and his private life became public entertainment. Unable to bear the publicity, the endless questions, and the demands on his time and energy, Lindbergh fled the United States and took refuge in England.

Goddard didn't want anything like that to happen to him.

# 7.

# The Race for Space

The country's best scientists were talking about the Goddard rocket. Professors were teaching their students about the possibilities of flight above the Earth's atmosphere. Astronomers and physicists were writing to Goddard with their suggestions. Engineers wanted to know about the design of his steering and propulsion systems.

Other letters came from foreign nations, many from Germany. After losing World War I, Germany had signed the Treaty of Versailles. The terms of the treaty were set down by the victorious Allies—Britain, France, and the United States—which had won the war. According to the treaty, the German government had to pay enormous sums of money to the Allies as reparations. Also, Germany was not allowed to manufacture military aircraft or other advanced weapons. But artillery rockets were no longer used as weapons, and the Versailles treaty had said nothing about them.

A German rocket society, the Verein für Raumschiffahrt, was formed in 1927. Three years later, during an economic depression, Germany's government granted the society fifty thousand dollars for rocket research. The scientists of the Verein set up a rocket testing ground near Berlin and began flying their own liquid-fuel rockets. Wernher von Braun, a brilliant young engineer, joined in the effort to build a high-altitude rocket—one that could be used not only for exploration, but also as a weapon.

Unlike Goddard, the Germans worked in teams, shared their discoveries and opinions, and published the results of their test flights in scientific magazines. Faced with many of the same problems as Goddard, they wrote to the professor and asked for his ideas. Goddard wrote back, always politely, to say that his research was "still in progress."

He still worked in private behind the closed doors of his workshop. Only he and the members of his crew were allowed to even look at the rockets and their systems. When the rockets were not being worked on or launched, they were securely locked away, out of sight. Goddard also asked his assistants to sign a pledge of secrecy.

Goddard would not cooperate with other scientists, German or American. He allowed only a few newspaper reporters to interview him and refused to publish the results of his tests. He answered detailed questions about the work with silence.

Why all the secrecy? He claimed that it was a matter of government orders. Yet the government wasn't helping him much.  He was not receiving enough from the Smithsonian, where Mr. Abbott was impatiently awaiting a successful high-altitude flight.  For building, testing, and launching, Goddard needed to pay for tubes and valves and tanks.  Fuel was expensive, and the crew had to be paid.

Goddard realized that he had to win a reliable private sponsor, a person or a company that wouldn't mind spending thousands—perhaps millions—on just the possibility of future space exploration.

In November 1929, the opportunity came.  Goddard received a call from Charles Lindbergh, who had read about the noisy flight over Auburn the past summer. Lindbergh himself had considered the possibility of flying beyond the earth.  But several scientists had told him that rocket flight was "impossible"—a word that he had heard often in 1927.  Lindbergh asked to visit Goddard's laboratory at Clark, where he could decide for himself.

Goddard agreed and gave the famous flier a warm welcome.  Much to Lindbergh's surprise, the professor showed him liquid-fueled rockets that had already flown. During the visit, Goddard also mentioned that full-time rocket research would probably cost around $25,000 a year.  Lindbergh promised to help if he could.

A few months later, Lindbergh called on Harry Guggenheim, the son of a wealthy businessman.  Guggenheim and his father, Daniel Guggenheim, were interested in the future of aviation—as a business.  In 1926 they had taken $3 million of the family's fortune to create the Guggenheim Fund for the Promotion of Aeronautics.  They used the money to help scientists and engineers working in the field.

Daniel Guggenheim invited Lindbergh to his home one night to talk about Robert Goddard.

"You believe these rockets have a future?" Guggenheim asked Lindbergh.

"Probably," Lindbergh replied.

"This professor of yours seems capable?"

"As far as I can tell, he knows more about rockets than anyone else in the country."

"Well, how much does he need?"

Lindbergh had to make a guess, so he used the figure

Goddard (center) with two of his main supporters, Harry Guggenheim (second from left) and Charles Lindbergh (third from right)

that Goddard had given him. "For a four-year project, $25,000 a year."

"Do you think it's worth $100,000?" Guggenheim demanded.

"Of course, it's taking a chance," said Lindbergh. "But if we're ever going beyond airplanes, we'll probably have to go to rockets."

Lindbergh described Goddard's successes as well as his failures. There was nothing certain about rocket flight, and the Guggenheims would be risking a lot of money. If Goddard failed, they would suffer a total loss. Even if he succeeded, they still might lose. Rockets might have no commercial possibility at all.

Nevertheless, Guggenheim decided to trust Lindbergh. The fund would donate $25,000 a year for four years to support Goddard's research. After two years, Goddard would have to report his results to a committee of nine men, including Lindbergh, Charles Abbott of the Smithsonian, and Wallace Atwood, the president of Clark University. These men, and the Guggenheims, would be closely watching Goddard's progress.

# At Mescalero Ranch

With Guggenheim's generous grant, Goddard could buy all the equipment and fuel he needed. He could pay himself and his assistants regular salaries, and he could move as far away as necessary to find a better location for his test flights. He had spent his entire life in Massachusetts, but now he was eager to begin the search for a new home—a place where his dream could finally come true.

Robert and Esther tried to imagine the ideal location. He needed a large, level, empty plain where the noise and smoke of rockets wouldn't disturb anybody—and where nobody would disturb him. The tests should be done on clear, dry days, when the rockets could be clearly seen, so he also needed a warm climate with plenty of sunshine. There should be no foggy days and not much wind. They also had to find a large house—four men and their families would be coming along to live and work under the same roof.

A meteorologist helped them search detailed climate maps of the United States. Finally they settled on a flat stretch of desert near the town of Roswell, in southeastern New Mexico. There was a single railroad line running through the town that they could use for big shipments. On the map, Roswell looked small and lonesome. But it also seemed an ideal place for rocket launches, and perhaps a much healthier spot for Goddard's frail lungs.

In the summer of 1930, the Goddards started out on the journey to New Mexico. Robert and Esther loaded their car and prepared for a long road trip. His assistants packed the launching tower and rocket parts into a freight car.

They followed two-lane highways through New England, the Appalachian Mountains, and the Midwest. As they crossed the Mississippi Valley and drew closer to New Mexico, the land turned from green cropland to open plains. Instead of cornfields and pastures, there were barbed-wire fences, drifting tumbleweeds, and dusty roads leading off to an empty horizon. The homes and shops of the Great Plains seemed to huddle close together for protection from the hot sun and flying dust.

After more than a week of driving and resting, the Goddards and the crew reached Roswell. They soon found an empty stone house on a stretch of nearby land known as Mescalero Ranch. The house stood at the end of a dirt road that left the main highway a few miles outside of town.

Goddard scouted the surrounding plains for a suitable launching site. He found bare cattle pastures and dry hillocks dotted with rocks, cactus, and spindly scrub. There were also stretches of flat, bare land deserted even by the desert snakes and scorpions. Cattle gates along the dirt roads kept the livestock from wandering off their owners' properties.

One day Goddard met Oscar White, a rancher who owned a spacious field about ten miles from Mescalero Ranch. The field was called Eden Valley, and it would be ideal for his work.

Goddard wasn't sure how a rancher would feel about rockets being launched on his land. But when he found out what Goddard was looking for, White agreed to help him. "I'd be glad to have you use the field, Doctor."

"I'm not sure if it's big enough," Goddard wondered aloud. For test flights, he needed at least three miles of level ground in every direction around the launch tower. There could be no people or buildings in the area where rockets would crash to earth.

"Well, it's a nice little field…about sixteen thousand acres," said White. This was big enough for Goddard, who was also happy to learn that White would charge him no rent. There was only one condition: While he was passing through, Goddard must leave the cattle gates just as he found them, whether open or closed.

Goddard then had his crew build a machine shop next to the house at Mescalero Ranch. The shop held work-benches, lathes, a writing desk, tools, and rocket parts. A special frame was set up on the grounds near the shop for static launch tests, in which the rocket wasn't supposed to move. Anchored by chains and heavy oil drums, the frame would hold the rockets in place during ignition.

With his static test frame built and a launching tower in place in Eden Valley, Goddard now had the chance to try out several new inventions. He worked on a more powerful motor, a new steering system, and a parachute that might help to break the rocket's fall.

The first static test took place on October 29, 1930.

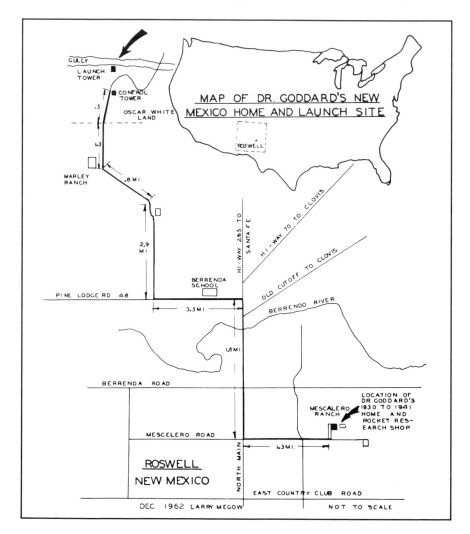

A new, larger combustion chamber, 5¾ inches in diameter, was fired several times, reaching a thrust of almost 300 pounds. On December 30 came the first launch of a new rocket, 11 feet long and weighing 33½ pounds without fuel. To feed the gasoline and liquid oxygen into the combustion chamber, Goddard had devised a tank of pressurized nitrogen gas, which would force the fuels more rapidly into the combustion chamber.

The rocket lifted 2,000 feet above the ground and reached a speed of 500 miles per hour. Goddard's rockets had never before reached this height or speed. But the strong thrust of the engines also made the rocket wobble during the flight. The rocket tilted to one side, and with a loud, sharp whistling sound, crashed back to earth about 1,000 feet away from the launch tower.

The launch of December 30 showed that the rocket still had problems. The most serious involved the higher temperature of the burning fuel, which was destroying the combustion chamber. Goddard would have to invent some way to cool the chamber. He also needed a better stabilizing system to keep the rocket upright during its flight.

In early 1931, a new cooling system was ready for testing. The device would spray a mixture of ignited gasoline and liquid oxygen into the chamber before lift-off. The mixture formed a sheet of cool liquid that protected the chamber's thin metal walls. Goddard called this "curtain cooling."

Through the spring and summer, he came up with other gadgets to improve the tests and the rocket flights. Using

Goddard with his wife, Esther, his crew, and Harry Guggenheim (far right) at the New Mexico launch tower.

Goddard's designs, the crew built a timer to control the release of the parachute, a remote-control launch system, and a new fuel pump.

The rocket was finally made ready for another flight

on September 29. Before dawn, Goddard and the shop crew drove to the launch site to prepare for the test. The rocket was unwrapped from its canvas covering and lifted into place between the guardrails in the launch tower. By remote control, Goddard started the fuels flowing into the combustion chamber. The countdown began.

The rocket roared and the tower trembled as the fuel ignited. Goddard threw a switch at the control panel, and the rocket began to rise. It reached 200 feet, picked up speed, and then began to lean over. Within seconds, it was flying along the ground like a giant artillery shell. It crossed 500 feet of desert and then hit the ground with a thunderous explosion.

Goddard and the crew rushed out to the crash site to inspect the wreckage. The gasoline tank had exploded, but the combustion chamber was still intact. Goddard concluded that the fuel pressure had been too low. Not enough fuel had been pumped into the combustion chamber, so the engine hadn't developed enough thrust to carry its weight. Gravity had quickly pulled it back to Earth.

Never discouraged by failure, Goddard tried to learn from every new problem that came along. This time, he would improve the fuel pump and then test it again. He would keep trying for higher altitudes and faster speeds. But he was still working alone, and getting no help from other scientists or inventors. Sometimes it seemed that his rockets, and his dreams, were coming back down to Earth.

# Reaching New Heights

More tests, and more work in the shop, were necessary. There were new problems to solve before Goddard could achieve the high-altitude flights that Lindbergh, Guggenheim, and his other sponsors were waiting for.

The motor was performing better, but the rocket still had no steering mechanism. It simply lifted off the ground, pushed upward by the burning fuel and sideways by the wind. At some point during every launch, it began to heel over and wobble out of control. When the force of gravity overcame lifting power, the rocket plummeted back toward the ground. It always crashed before running out of fuel.

To solve this problem, Goddard attached four vanes—flat sheets of metal—to the bottom of the rocket, in the path of the exhaust. The spinning gyroscope inside the rocket was linked to the vanes. If the rocket began to wobble to one side, the gyroscope would lean to the other side. This turned one of the vanes into the exhaust, stabilizing the rocket in the air the way a rudder steers a boat through the water.

Goddard put this "gyrostabilizer" system to a test on April 19, 1932. The gyroscope began spinning, the fuel ignited, and the rocket began its ascent. The flight was short, but straight. After the crash, Goddard carefully inspected the steering vanes. One of them was hot to the touch—proof that the system had worked. The gyroscope had pushed this vane into the exhaust and straightened the rocket's path.

Goddard prepared his new system for another test flight in May. This time, the fuels burned clean through the walls of the combustion chamber. The exhaust nozzle hissed and sputtered as the pressure in the chamber fell to zero. The parachute popped out of the nose, then slowly wafted down the side of the rocket. There would be no flight.

Dejected, Goddard took the rocket back to the workshop for an inspection. It seemed that the many ingenious devices he had invented were not cooperating. When one worked, the others would fail. More tests were needed, but the committee back East was waiting.

That summer, Goddard had to make a report on his progress. He traveled to Washington, where he asked the members of the Guggenheim committee for two more years. The members of the committee listened. They were impressed by Goddard's patience and resourcefulness. If anyone could succeed at this project, Goddard would.

But there were problems. The Guggenheim fortune was shrinking. The Great Depression, the worst economic crisis in the country's history, was going on, and the family had lost millions when the stock market crashed. For the time being, there would be no more money from the Guggenheim foundation for rocket research.

Goddard would have to fire his assistants, lock up the house and workshop, and move back to Massachusetts. Luckily, his old teaching job was still open at Clark University. While the workshop in Roswell gathered dust and cobwebs, he again became a modest physics professor. His plans and his rockets were put aside.

Goddard still worried about the new systems he had invented for the rocket. Possibly they could be modified for use in cars or airplanes. Since they weren't yet patented, another engineer could legally copy the devices and produce them in a factory. Goddard would gain nothing.

To stop this from happening, the professor took two of his designs down to the office of Charles T. Hawley, the lawyer who had helped him with his first patents. The first was his device for "curtain cooling"; the other was his gyroscopic steering system.

Goddard also wanted to patent a design for a new type of engine that he had designed the year before. This device used air that passed into the engine and was compressed between metal blades. The compressed air then mixed with fuel in a combustion chamber, where small explosions took place at the rate of six hundred per second. The igniting fuel forced exhaust gases to the rear and provided the engine's forward thrust. This "resonance chamber," as Goddard called it, was an early type of jet engine.

After Hawley applied for the patents, they were quickly approved and published. Copies of the designs were sold in the United States as well as Germany.

In 1934 the Guggenheim Foundation decided to again provide Goddard with money for his research. Esther and Robert and the crew headed back to the high plains near Roswell. This time, the committee had voted to grant eighteen thousand dollars. But this time the committee also wanted to see progress—a successful flight, if possible.

Goddard built a larger rocket for testing in 1935. This model was 15 feet long and weighed about 85 pounds without fuel. The rocket now had a solid outer skin of duralumin. The shell covered the rocket from its tail vanes to its nose cone. It provided a smoother flight and protected the inner parts of the rocket. A new remote-control ignition system was set up, and the gyroscopic steering was placed on board.

The rocket was first tested on March 28. After ignition, the craft began to wobble as it cleared the tower. But the spinning gyroscope and the steering vanes steadied the rocket, and it reached a height of 4,800 feet. As the fuel gave out, the rocket lost its balance, heeled to one side, and smashed into the ground 2 miles away. For 20 seconds, the gyrostabilizer had worked.

During a test in May, the rocket reached 7,500 feet, one-fifth of the way to the stratosphere (the second layer of Earth's atmosphere). It was the highest altitude Goddard had ever achieved. He was getting closer to real spaceflight—but he was still very far away.

# 10.

# A Secret
# Science

In September 1935, Esther and Robert Goddard readied the house and workshop for a very important visit. Charles Lindbergh and Harry Guggenheim had accepted their invitation to come to New Mexico to witness a rocket launch. They arrived on the twenty-second, and spent that evening and much of the night talking excitedly about aviation and spaceflight.

Worried about problems and accidents, Goddard had prepared two rockets for the demonstration. If one broke down, another would be available. On September 23, as Lindbergh and Guggenheim watched, the crew raised the first rocket in its launch tower. The visitors took shelter as the gasoline and liquid oxygen began to flow through the rocket's valves. After a short countdown, Goddard threw the switches for ignition.

Nothing happened. The rocket's igniter had failed.

The professor set up the second rocket. Another countdown began. The rocket sat, unmoving, as the heat of the ignited fuels burned out the combustion chamber.

Robert and Esther Goddard at Mescalero Ranch in 1937

Two tests, and two failures. Guggenheim and Lindbergh were disappointed, but they encouraged Goddard to keep trying. They understood that there would always be problems to work out, mistakes and failures to overcome. They left New Mexico with a promise to keep supporting Goddard in his work.

The two men had many conversations about Goddard's work after their return to the East. Lindbergh, who had earned the nickname the "Lone Eagle" for his solo flight across the Atlantic, knew many scientists who liked to work alone. But he also worried that Goddard's own secrecy was slowing down the rocket's progress.

Guggenheim was becoming impatient. He wanted real progress, progress he could see, hear, and feel. Like Charles Abbott at the Smithsonian, he was eager to read about a record-breaking, high-altitude rocket flight. The best way to achieve this, he believed, was for Goddard to begin cooperating with other scientists.

The two men wanted Goddard to share his secrets, at least with the institution that had done so much to help him. They persuaded Goddard to pack one of his rockets and ship it to the Smithsonian museum in Washington D.C. The rocket would become public property, but Goddard would not allow the public to see it. With the wooden crate holding the rocket Goddard had sent along a typewritten note:

"It is understood that this is not to be placed on exhibition until requested by me or, in the event of my death, by Mr. Harry F. Guggenheim and Colonel Charles A. Lindbergh."

After the rocket arrived, the Smithsonian director ordered his staff to build a false wall in one of the exhibition rooms. The rocket was hidden behind the wall, safe and secret in its wooden crate, for many years. Although

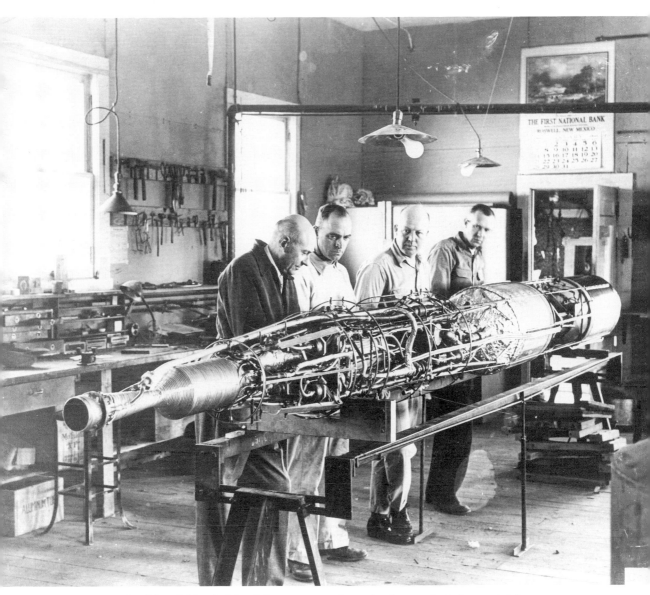

Goddard (far left) with crew members in the rocket shop at Mescalero Ranch. This rocket is now displayed at the Smithsonian.

the rocket was now public property, visitors to the museum didn't even know it was there.

Goddard also agreed to write up another report for the Smithsonian. The ten-page paper, "Liquid Propellant

Rocket Development," covered his progress from 1930 until 1935. The Smithsonian published it in March 1936.

The paper described Goddard's new rocket devices in a general way, with few details. Nevertheless, strange things happened to the report before it was published. A proof of the article that had been sent to Goddard disappeared in the mail. The professor also noticed that someone was opening letters and packages before they reached his mailbox in Roswell. He never found out who was tampering with his mail, but he had a notion that, somehow, foreign scientists were responsible.

At the same time, he was building a new model, the "L" series. The L-series rockets weighed about 200 pounds before fueling—the largest he had yet designed. But they also gave Goddard new problems. The nitrogen tank was now too heavy, and through the spring and summer the L-series rockets sputtered to meager altitudes. Goddard and his crew sweated and struggled to improve the rocket, but they had little success.

Goddard decided to take a break and think things over. His crew left for vacations, and he traveled to California. There he visited Dr. Robert Millikan, the head of the physics department at the California Institute of Technology. Cal Tech students were working on their own rockets under the direction of Theodor von Karman, an immigrant from Hungary. By the mid-1930s, the school had become an important center of aeronautical research.

Millikan told Goddard that the problems of rocket technology were too complex for one man, working alone, to solve. Cooperation and teamwork, he claimed, were

Dr. Robert Millikan

necessary. Millikan would soon put this idea into practice, whether Goddard liked it or not. After the meeting, he asked Frank Malina, one of his students, to drive out to Mescalero Ranch to look around and ask questions.

Goddard returned to New Mexico, still determined to guard his creation from the prying eyes of the outside world. When Malina showed up in late August, the Goddards politely greeted their surprise guest. But Goddard gave short answers to Malina's questions, and kept his inventions firmly under wraps. The Goddard rocket would remain his own.

# A Threat
# from Germany

Between 1936 and 1939, Charles Lindbergh paid several visits to Germany, where he toured the country's new air bases and busy weapons factories. German leaders were defying the Treaty of Versailles by rebuilding their armed forces. They worried little about what the Allies might do in response. Instead, they were anxious to show Lindbergh and the world their growing military strength.

In 1933, Adolf Hitler and the Nazi party had taken control of Germany. Hitler ordered new ships, planes, tanks, and artillery pieces. Germany also had a rocket program. The country's best scientists, including Wernher von Braun, were working on a liquid-fueled craft called the Repulsor. The Repulsor was not an exploratory rocket or a commercial enterprise. It was a weapon. And the Repulsor's designers, laboratories, and test sites were strictly off limits to Colonel Lindbergh.

In the United States, the Guggenheim Foundation was now supporting several rocket researchers, including Theodor von Karman at Cal Tech. Harry Guggenheim

Theodor von Karman teaching at Cal Tech

asked Professor Goddard to come east to meet these other scientists. Goddard could talk openly to them about the problems of rocket flight.

Goddard agreed. At the meeting, he spoke about his discoveries and his successes and failures. Perhaps, he suggested, Cal Tech could take over the design of some parts of his rocket.

But Dr. von Karman and the others wanted to work with Goddard on the entire machine, from nose to tail. By working together, they claimed, they could perfect steering, combustion, fuel pumps, and all the other complex components needed in a high-altitude vehicle.

Goddard did not agree. He would keep his rocket hidden from view in New Mexico and his inventions a closely guarded secret. He needed no partners—just assistants who would carry out his directions and help create the parts he needed. He believed that he could learn more from his own failures than from the suggestions and opinions of others. The meeting broke up, and the scientists went their separate ways.

By now, Goddard realized that the rockets he had already built would never fly beyond the atmosphere. Although these models were able to fly faster than the speed of sound, only much larger rockets carrying much more fuel would be able to attain escape velocity and reach space.

To get larger rockets into the air, Goddard needed more pressure in the combustion chamber. For two years, he worked on a new type of fuel pump. On August 1, 1940, the crew launched the pump for the first time. The rocket lifted from the tower, reached 300 feet, turned on its side, and crashed. The test looked like a failure, but Dr. Goddard was satisfied. For a few seconds, his new pump had worked.

# 12.

# The Last
# Launches

In September 1939, Adolf Hitler ordered his army to invade Poland. Germany's modern tanks and planes swept across the Polish frontier to destroy cities and factories. The defenders fought back with outdated rifles, cannons, and soldiers on horseback. While Germany attacked from the west, the Soviet Union attacked from the east. Within a few weeks, Poland was defeated and occupied by the German army. Britain and France declared war against Germany, and World War II was underway.

The U.S. government didn't enter the conflict right away, but many military leaders wanted to prepare the American forces for war. They formed the National Defense Research Committee to investigate new inventions for possible military use. Many leading scientists were asked to join the committee.

The coming of the war changed Goddard's mind about

cooperating with other scientists on his rocket research. He wanted to be useful. But unfortunately, he had a reputation as a man too secretive to be of use to the government. The members of the National Defense Research Committee did not invite him to join them, and Goddard stayed in New Mexico.

He was certain that liquid-fueled rockets would make powerful weapons. They could be launched from planes or used on the ground against tanks or fortifications. They could carry explosives across great distances, perhaps hundreds of miles, and could be used against cities and factories. He suspected that German scientists, perhaps using Goddard's own designs, were already building such rockets.

He wrote letters to the army, the navy, and David Walsh, a senator from Massachusetts. He also wrote to Clarence Hickman, who had helped Goddard develop and demonstrate the mobile tube launcher back in 1918. He forgot about spies and secrecy. Now he only wanted a chance to show what his rockets could do with a little more time and testing. Finally, in 1940, the Army Air Corps asked Goddard to come to Washington and present his ideas.

The officers of the Army Air Corps listened while Goddard explained how his rockets worked. There were a few questions, and then the busy officers brought the meeting to an end. General George Brett asked Goddard to write up his ideas and send them back to the Corps as a formal proposal. They would then get back to him about a research contract. If Goddard wanted to make

Goddard prepares to launch a test rocket. The controls for firing, launching, and stopping are on the table beside him.

progress, Brett added, he would have to go through the proper channels.

After the meeting, Goddard returned to Mescalero Ranch. He wrote a proposal, sent it off to Washington, and waited for a response. For several months, nothing happened. In the meantime, Germany was attacking France, Norway, Denmark, and the Netherlands. Hitler also made an alliance with Japan. The war was spreading to North Africa and the Pacific, and it seemed to Goddard and to the rest of the world that Germany could not be stopped.

Through the winter and spring, Goddard and his crew

continued their work. From the military there was no answer, and no contract. In May 1941, Goddard launched a 22-foot, 500-pound rocket. It flew about 250 feet above the tower before crashing. Although he didn't know it, this would be Goddard's last launch.

Finally, in the summer of 1941, the U.S. Navy asked Goddard to begin work on jet-assisted takeoff devices, or JATOs. The Navy saw that jet engines, with their fast takeoffs, could be used to help its planes clear the very short runways of aircraft carriers. Goddard signed a contract that would pay him enough money to hire several new workers at Mescalero Ranch. That fall, the crew began testing the jet devices in New Mexico.

Goddard knew that he would have to leave behind his dream of spaceflight, at least until the war was over. For now, he was making a contribution to his country. He could stay at Mescalero Ranch and put his imagination to work on a practical goal. He was satisfied that he was doing the right thing.

Shortly after the testing began, the Japanese air force attacked Pearl Harbor, an important naval and air base in Hawaii. On the next day, President Franklin Roosevelt declared war on Germany and Japan. For the United States, World War II had begun.

# JATOs, PBYs, and V-2s

The work on JATOs was now a top priority. Early in 1942, the navy ordered Goddard to move his experiments to the Naval Engineering Experimental Station at Annapolis, Maryland. Goddard would have to move away from Mescalero Ranch, probably for the rest of the war.

At Annapolis, Goddard discovered that a team of scientists, engineers, and test pilots was already hard at work on JATOs. His task would be to get the device ready for use on a PBY, a seaplane that could take off from either water or dry land. The nearby Severn River would serve as both a testing site and an observation station for Navy officers.

After months of further work and preparation, Goddard finally had the JATO device ready for a test flight on September 23. Despite all of his precautions, Goddard was worried. For the first time, there would be a live pilot flying one of his inventions. A flaw in the engine or the materials, or one of his own miscalculations, could cause a deadly accident.

To be safe, he had installed several devices that would shut down the engine in case of an emergency. Before the test, he boarded a small rescue boat that was brought to the middle of the river. While he watched the plane prepare for its flight, he held a remote control radio. If necessary, the radio could signal the crew of the plane to stop the test.

Lieutenant Charles Fischer and his crew climbed into the PBY. Fischer taxied the plane along the river's gentle waves to the takeoff point. The JATO engine was revved up—and then stopped.

Five times Goddard's safety devices cut off the engine and stopped the test. Finally, on the sixth try, the PBY rumbled into the air and flew several thousand feet along the river. The plane splashed down to a smooth landing. Fischer turned and prepared for another takeoff.

Then something went wrong. Goddard tried to order the pilot to abort the test but discovered that the remote control radio had stopped working. The plane struggled into the air when the heat inside the motor burned through a tank of liquid oxygen. The lox—the dangerous stuff that had safely powered so many of Goddard's own rocket launches—burst into flames.

With its tail alight, the PBY began to wobble and lose altitude. The pilot brought the burning plane back down to the water as Goddard's rescue boat rushed to meet it. The tail kept burning as the professor helped to pull the pilot and the crew to safety.

Although the PBY had nearly crashed, its jet engine had lifted it into the air at high speed, over a short takeoff distance, just as designed. Goddard continued the tests, always taking care that his safety devices and his radio were in good working order.

The military continued its development of JATO devices, but Goddard's idea for rockets used as weapons was ignored. Instead, the government was building a top-secret bomb in the New Mexico desert, not far from Mescalero Ranch. Instead of gunpowder or TNT, the bomb used uranium, a rare chemical element. A chain reaction of uranium atoms would touch off an immense explosion. In an instant, this "atomic" weapon could flatten an entire city. No rockets were needed, because these atom bombs could be dropped from airplanes. Many scientists believed that the device would force the enemy to surrender and end the war.

In Germany, meanwhile, scientists were also thinking of the possible use of atomic weapons. But they had decided that the use of atomic power in a bomb was impossible, because too much uranium would be needed to set off the chain reaction. Instead, Wernher von Braun and his colleagues were testing rocket-powered bombs at Peenemünde, a secret base on the coast of the Baltic Sea.

In June 1944, as the United States and its allies were invading Europe, Germany began launching explosive rockets at England from the coast of France. These "V-1s" were about 25 feet long and powered by a shutter-type engine similar to the jet device Goddard had patented in 1934. The V-1 was fired from a concrete ramp. Its engine shut down in flight, allowing the rocket to glide to its target under the force of gravity. More than twenty thousand were used during the war. The English called them "buzz bombs" because of the frightening buzzing noise the V-1 made while flying over their cities.

When he read a description of the V-1, Goddard realized that the Germans had copied the resonance chamber that he had patented in 1932. Since patents are public information, the design could legally be published. A German aviation magazine, *Flugsport,* had done just this in 1939.

A German V-1 "buzz bomb" approaching a target in southern England

Members of Goddard's crew in the Roswell shop with a rocket that Goddard described as very similar to the German V-2

But the Germans were also building an even more dangerous weapon called the V-2. These rockets were 47 feet long and weighed 9,000 pounds without fuel. They flew at a speed of 3,600 miles per hour and reached a height of 60 miles. Neither anti-aircraft shells nor planes could reach that height. There was no defense against the V-2.

Adolf Hitler believed that the V-2 was an unstoppable weapon that would save his country from defeat. The Germans launched more than four thousand of them. Although many missed their targets, the ones that hit populated areas of England destroyed entire city blocks and sparked devastating fires.

In March 1945, an unexploded V-2 rocket was found. The rocket was shipped to the United States, where Dr.

German rocket engineer Wernher von Braun after World War II

Goddard carefully examined it. Inside the V-2 he found turbine fuel pumps, a system of "curtain cooling," and gyroscopic stabilizers. Liquid oxygen and alcohol fueled the weapons. The V-2 looked like a copy of the rockets Goddard had been designing and testing for the past twenty years. But instead of reaching for the moon, these rockets landed on cities and people with nearly a ton of high explosive.

The V-2 did not save Germany from defeat. In May 1945, German leaders formally surrendered to the Allies, one week after Hitler committed suicide. Von Braun and the other rocket scientists were captured and questioned about their wonder weapons. They explained their weapons and systems in great detail, but denied that they had stolen Goddard's rocket design.

Goddard continued his work at Annapolis until the end of the war. But the damp climate of the region worsened his health. By the summer of 1943, his lungs and throat were in such poor shape that he could hardly speak. He was forced to write out instructions to his assistants.

In June 1945, Goddard developed cancer of the throat. Doctors had to remove his larynx to stop the cancer from spreading. Goddard never recovered from the operation. He died on August 10, just a few days after the United States dropped the world's first atomic bombs on Hiroshima and Nagasaki, Japan.

# Afterword

After the war, Esther Goddard and Charles Hawley applied for many more patents in Robert Goddard's name. The U.S. Patent Office granted Robert Goddard, before and after his death, a total of 214 patents. The government used many of these inventions and designs for its own rocket programs, without paying for them. Finally, in 1960, the United States agreed to pay $1 million to Esther Goddard and the Guggenheim Foundation for the rights to Goddard's patents.

The professor's dream of high-altitude spaceflight and exploration would not be achieved until the late 1950s. In October 1957, the Soviet Union launched the Sputnik satellite. In the next year the United States sent the satellite Explorer to a height of 600 miles. Wernher von Braun led the team at the California Institute of Technology that designed the satellite.

By the 1960s, both nations were putting astronauts into earth orbit by launching rockets fueled by liquid hydrogen and liquid oxygen. Gyroscopes steered the rockets through space, and multiple stages were used to lighten the weight of the rockets after they reached orbit. These spacecraft were distant relatives of the rockets Goddard had been designing and testing thirty years before in the New Mexico desert.

The German V-2s had taught the Soviet Union and the United States an important lesson about military rockets, which can carry atomic weapons as well as ordinary high-explosive charges. After Germany's defeat in 1945, Hermann Oberth and Wernher von Braun worked with American scientists at the White Sands Proving Ground in New Mexico to build and test new, more powerful atomic weapons.

By the 1960s, the United States and the Soviet Union had built enormous arsenals of nuclear Intercontinental Ballistic Missiles, or ICBMs. The nuclear devices within these weapons are much more powerful than the bombs used on Hiroshima and Nagasaki. The ICBMs now sit below ground in remote launching sites, targeted and ready for use.

In the meantime, rockets also became a vehicle for peaceful modern exploration. In 1969, the Apollo 11 spacecraft carried Neil Armstrong, Michael Collins, and Buzz Aldrin to the moon. Later, unoccupied probes landed on Mars and Venus. Space shuttles and telescopes have been launched into orbit far above the earth. Europe and the United States have built satellites for telecommunications, for photography, and for weather forecasting. All these devices have one thing in common: they're flying into space on Goddard rockets.

# Notes

page 18

Many inventors would propose similar trains in the years after Goddard wrote his school essay. In Switzerland, engineers are now planning an underground train system that will run beneath the Swiss Alps, a mountain range that stretches across the country. The Swissmetro, as it is called, will be powered by electromagnets in an airless tunnel. Just as Goddard proposed, this design will eliminate air resistance and friction.

page 19

Robert Goddard applied for a patent on a vacuum tube oscillator on August 1, 1912. He designed the device to produce electrical impulses, or oscillations. Several other scientists were working on the same device at about the same time. In 1914, an inventor named Lee DeForest patented a vacuum tube oscillator that produced a clear, steady audio signal. The signal could carry sounds, music, and voices through the air.

This was an important event in the development of radio, but Goddard had little interest in the subject. Instead, he turned to rocketry. Meanwhile, DeForest's patents were bought by companies that sold radio transmitters. While Goddard struggled to win small grants to fund his rocket research, DeForest earned a fortune from his radio patents.

page 29

Goddard's recoilless tube launcher later became the bazooka, a weapon first used by U.S. soldiers in North Africa during World War II. The bazooka weighed about 10 pounds and was light enough to be fired from the shoulder. Since it was open at both ends, the soldier using it was not affected by "kick," or recoil.

Goddard did not patent his tube-launcher and received no payment or royalties from the making of bazookas.

## page 34

During the 1920s and 1930s, Oberth became a hero of German rocket scientists, who claimed that his ideas and designs were much more practical for space exploration than Goddard's. But Oberth never launched a test rocket.

Neither Oberth nor Goddard was the first to propose space exploration by rockets. In 1903, Konstantin Tsiolkovsky, a Russian schoolteacher, published "Investigation of Space by Means of Rockets." Tsiolkovsky described the use of liquid fuels and multistage rockets, but he never built a working rocket model. Using the theories of Tsiolkovsky and other Russian pioneers, the Soviet Union beat the United States in the race to reach space by launching the Sputnik satellite in 1957.

## page 64

In fact, a German by the name of Gustav Guellich *did* spy on Robert Goddard. A native of Munich, Germany, Guellich arrived in the United States in 1932 and found work in a shipyard in Kearny, New Jersey. He later joined a spy ring organized by the Abwehr, Germany's espionage agency, in New York City.

Guellich sent in detailed reports, as well as ship blueprints that he obtained at the Kearny shipyard. In 1936, he also began reporting on Goddard's rockets. Guellich was uncertain of the rockets' purpose, however. When the Abwehr leaders questioned him about this, he told them that Goddard was developing a new rocket guidance system for torpedoes.

# Glossary

**combustion chamber:** a cylinder in which fuels are mixed and burned to provide thrust to a rocket

**curtain cooling:** a system of forcing cool liquids into the combustion chamber before ignition. This lessens the high temperatures that occur during combustion and can damage or destroy the combustion chamber. Goddard first used a combination of gasoline and liquid oxygen for his curtain cooling system.

**escape velocity:** the speed that an object must reach in order to escape the pull of gravity above Earth—about 25,000 miles per hour

**gunpowder:** a mixture of explosive substances that, when ignited, propel an object such as a bullet, an artillery shell, or a firework rocket. A common gunpowder mixture is charcoal, sulfur, and potassium nitrate; this mixture is also known as black powder.

**gyroscope:** a device that is used to stabilize rockets and airplanes. A gyroscope includes a spinning wheel that resists any change of its position. When linked with a steering system, it can help rockets fly straight and on course.

**hydrogen:** a chemical element that, when used in liquid form, is the lightest and most efficient fuel source for rocket flight

**oxygen:** a light chemical element that, in liquid form, serves as an oxidant. Fire needs oxygen to keep burning. In space, where there is no air or oxygen, an oxidant provides the oxygen necessary for the burning of rocket fuel.

**recoil:** the backward force of a gun or cannon after it has been fired

**static tests:** a method of firing rockets while keeping them firmly secured to the ground. In a static test, the rocket designer can closely examine the performance of the rocket's engine.

**stratosphere:** an upper layer of the earth's atmosphere, extending from about 7 to 30 miles above sea level

**thrust:** the force generated by a rocket engine, measured in pounds

**turbine:** an engine that is powered by the flow of a substance, such as water or air. Jet turbines take in air, and for that reason, they cannot work in space, where there is no air.

# Bibliography

Bibliography

Farley, Karen Clafford. *Robert H. Goddard.* Englewood Cliffs, New Jersey: Silver Burdett Press, 1991.

Goddard, Robert H. *The Papers of Robert H. Goddard.* New York: McGraw-Hill Book Co., 1963.

Lampton, Christopher. *Wernher von Braun.* New York: Franklin Watts, 1988.

Lehman, Milton. *This High Man: The Life of Robert H. Goddard.* New York: Farrar, Strauss, and Co., 1963.

Pendray, G. Edward. *The Coming Age of Rocket Power.* New York and London: Harper and Brothers, 1945.

Quackenbush, Robert. *The Boy Who Dreamed of Rockets: How Robert H. Goddard Became the Father of the Space Age.* New York: Parents Magazine Press, 1978.

Verral, Charles Spain. *Robert Goddard, Father of the Space Age.* Englewood Cliffs, New Jersey: Prentice-Hall, Inc., 1963.

von Braun, Wernher, with Frederick L. Ordway III and Dave Dooling. *Space Travel: A History.* New York: Harper and Row Publishers, 1985.

Winter, Frank H. *Rockets into Space.* Cambridge, Massachusetts: Harvard University Press, 1990.

# Index

Illustrations are reproduced through the courtesy of: Goddard Collection, Clark University Archives, front cover (inset), pp. 2, 6, 10, 15, 19, 22, 33, 36, 40, 47, 52, 54, 61, 63, 71, 77; Bettmann, p. 24; UPI/Bettmann, pp. 34, 76, 78; Smithsonian Institution, p. 42; Archives, California Institute of Technology, pp. 65, 67.